BOOK TWO

38 SELECTED DUETS

FOR TWO TRUMPETS
(Or Cornets)

(Intermediate – Advanced)

Compiled and Edited by

JAY ARNOLD

Advancing from Book One, consisting of 78 Selected Duets for Two Trumpets (or Cornets) in easy to intermediate form, we now present 38 duets of four masters of this form of composition, with arrangements of an intermediate to an advance grade. These duets will be of great value to the repertoires of players who have acquired proficiency in the intermediate grades.

CONTENTS

	Page
PIERRE-FRANCOIS CLODOMIR	
12 Duets, Opus 15	2
HERMANN PIETZSCH	
14 Duets	26
DOMENICO GATTI	
9 Duets	42
SAINT-JACOME	
3 Duets	67

TWELVE DUETS
Opus 15

PIERRE-FRANCOIS CLODOMIR

TRUMPET II

Allegretto moderato

TWELVE DUETS

Opus 15

TRUMPET I

PIERRE-FRANCOIS CLODOMIR

TRUMPET II

Allegretto grazioso

Allegretto grazioso

Andantino

4

Allegro non troppo

5

Allegro non troppo

5

TRUMPET II

TRUMPET I

Tempo di Marcia

7

Allegretto

8

Moderato

9

TRUMPET II

Allegro con moto

10

11

Tempo di Bolero

12

Tempo di Bolero

12

FOURTEEN DUETS

TRUMPET II

HERMANN PIETZSCH

FOURTEEN DUETS

TRUMPET I

HERMANN PIETZSCH

TRUMPET II

TRUMPET I

TRUMPET II

TRUMPET I

TRUMPET II

Allegro moderato

9

Allegro moderato

NINE DUETS

DOMENICO GATTI

46

Allegretto

pp con grazia ed espressivo

Tempo I

Poco più mosso

Allegretto

53

Andante con moto

Andante cantabile

7

61

Maestoso

THREE DUETS

SAINT-JACOME

68

70

col canto

D.S. to 2nd Var.

3rd VAR.

mf

tr

D.S. to 3rd Var.

4th VAR.

mf

tr

5th VAR. Minore
Più lento.

D.S. to 4th Var.

Cadenza
ad lib.

col canto

Tempo I

Moderato leggiero e grazioso

RONDO Scherzando